by Isabel Thomas

Toxic!

Proteins are an essential part of all living things. Your own body contains over 100 000 different kinds of proteins.

Some animals produce toxic proteins which can harm other animals.

How many toxic animals can you think of? So far, scientists have made a list of more than 200 000!

Some toxic animals are poisonous. Others are venomous. What is the difference?

Poisonous animals contain toxic proteins. They can only harm another animal if they are touched or eaten. Toxic proteins often taste disgusting, which helps keep **predators** away.

poisonous

Many frogs have toxic skin.

Venomous animals deliver toxic proteins into another animal on purpose. Many use their venom to catch **prey**.

venomous

Some snakes inject venom through large, hollow fangs.

A wasp's sting delivers venom.

Floating Fiends

There are not many places to hide from predators in the sea. Many sea creatures produce poison for self-defence.

Tiger puffer fish make one of the world's most dangerous poisons.

poisonous

Box jellyfish are covered with tiny, venom-tipped stingers. When a small animal is stung, its muscles stop working properly. This enables the jellyfish to **seize** the prey.

venomous

Sea nettles are huge jellyfish with a painful sting. However, not every animal is affected by their venom. Penguins have been spotted feasting on sea nettles!

venomous

Penguins have defences against jellyfish toxins. Jellyfish of all kinds seem to be an important food for penguins.

Harpoon Hunters

Cone snails catch prey using a tiny **harpoon** tipped with deadly venom. The harpoon moves in and out of the shell at high speed.

Geographic cone snail venom is a mixture of hundreds of different toxins. It kills fish instantly. The geographic cone snail can then eat its meal at its own speed.

A whole geographic cone snail may contain enough venom to kill 700 people!

Red Alert!

poisonous

Toxic animals lurk on land, too. Beware of bright animals!

poisonous

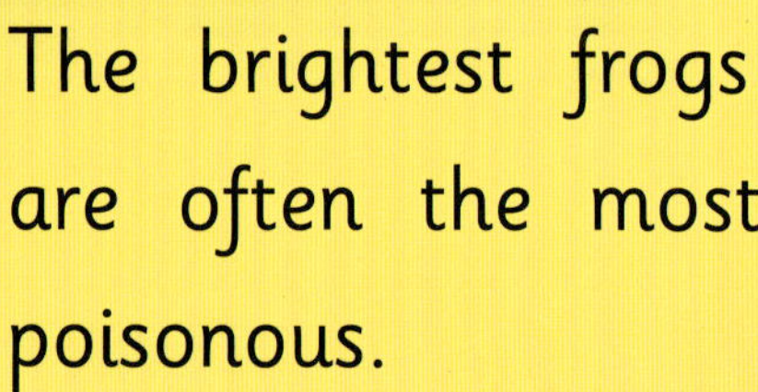

The brightest frogs are often the most poisonous.

Each bump on this moth caterpillar is armed with droplets of poison!

Shocking pink dragon millipedes don't need to hide. Their spines are armed with a poisonous liquid. Red advertises danger.

poisonous

When threatened, toxic yellow-bellied toads flip onto their backs. Their bright bellies persuade predators to stay away.

poisonous

Snake Bites

Not all toxic animals look bright.

inland taipan snake

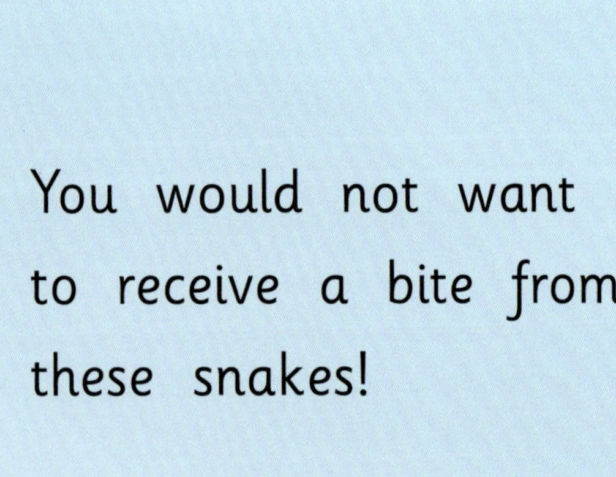

You would not want to receive a bite from these snakes!

red milk snake

Taipan snakes that look dull have the strongest venom of any land snakes. Each drop of venom could kill 100 people.

A bite will always prove deadly unless it is treated quickly. Luckily, taipans are shy and like to stay underground.

venomous

Some snakes are bright to deceive other animals.

Predators cannot tell which one is poisonous and which one is safe to eat. They leave both snakes alone.

These birds use the same trick!

Mind the Mammal

venomous

Mammals may look cute and furry, but a few are armed with toxic venom!

A slow loris's venom makes it smell like a cobra snake, keeping predators away.

Solenodons inject venom into prey through sharp, hollow teeth, like snakes.

venomous

Male platypuses have spurs on their back legs. **Rivals** might receive a painful stab.

Toxic Defences

Like the penguins at sea, many mammals have defences against toxic animals.

Honey badgers can survive snake bites that would kill an elephant. They make proteins that **deactivate** the snake venom.

Many toxic animals also make **antidote** proteins, which deactivate their own venom. This means toxic animals can help us.

Snakes are 'milked' for their venom to make antidotes. These antidotes help to save many people's lives.

Saving Lives

Some animal toxins are even used to make medicines that keep people healthy.

Cone snail venom has inspired scientists to improve medicines for **diabetes**.

Scientists are still discovering the secrets of toxic animals. They may be some of nature's most amazing creatures.

Glossary

antidote: a substance that stops poison or venom from causing harm

deactivate: to stop something from working

diabetes: a condition that causes high blood sugar

harpoon: a long, sharp weapon

predators: animals that hunt other animals for food

prey: an animal that is hunted by another animal

proteins: nutrients that help animals to grow

rivals: competitors who want the same things as you

seize: to grab or take hold of

Index